NO ONE TO WASTE

A Report to Public Decision-Makers and Community College Leaders

ROBERT H. McCABE

The National Study of Community College Remedial Education

Community College Press®
a division of the American Association of Community Colleges
Washington, D.C.

The National Study of Community College Remedial Education is a project of The League for Innovation in the Community College in conjunction with the American Association of Community Colleges, with assistance from the Education Commission of the States and support from the Pew Charitable Trusts. Robert H. McCabe directed the study.

The opinions expressed in this report are those of the author and do not necessarily reflect the views of the Pew Charitable Trusts.

The American Association of Community Colleges (AACC) is the primary advocacy organization for the nation's community colleges. The association represents 1,100 two-year, associate degree-granting institutions and some 10 million students. AACC provides leadership and service in five key areas: policy initiatives, advocacy, research, education services, and coordination/networking.

Printed in the United States of America.
ISBN 0-87117-330-1

CONTENTS

FIGURES

TABLES

PREFACE

For most of my life, I have worked in a community college and lived in a community where the population has changed from predominantly white non-Hispanic to a "majority minority." I have experienced the joy of seeing people overcome seemingly insurmountable obstacles to move themselves and their families into the mainstream of American life. I have learned that the educationally underprepared are not undertalented. I have also despaired as I witnessed many people trapped by life circumstances into a seemingly inescapable underclass.

As we begin a new century, it is clear that our nation is being transformed just as my home community has been. The American spirit values every person, and the nation benefits when everyone's talents are developed. At times, an extra effort must be put forth to help and allow people to reach their potential, or the whole nation suffers.

The purpose of the National Study of Community College Remedial Education is to enhance understanding of the role of remedial education in our new national environment. The study and this work are dedicated to improving the effectiveness of remedial education, a critical component of American higher education.

Preparing for a Changing World

Information technology is transforming the world at a breathtaking pace. The economy will be built on knowledge industries that need highly skilled employees. But many young Americans do not have the competency for 21st-century employment. Eighty percent of new jobs will require some postsecondary education; unfortunately, only 42 percent of students leave high school with the necessary skills to begin college-level work. A third of those who enter college are underprepared.

While students work to develop fundamental educational competence, businesses grapple with a drastically underskilled workforce. Industry leaders report that between 20 and 40 percent of new hires are underqualified for their positions. As a result, they are looking outside the United States for answers, pressuring Congress to issue more visas to import skilled foreign workers.

New Directions for Public Education

More than ever, our future depends on education. Public school performance must be dramatically improved, and more students must graduate from high school with skills to enter college. America's changing demographics, however, threaten to overwhelm an already strained educational system. The country's growing populations are minorities—principally Hispanics and other undereducated immigrants. They are disproportionately poor, and this condition correlates to underpreparation at every educational level. The children of minorities often begin school several steps behind, many times without essential family support.

State school reformers are addressing educational progress with high expectations but limited success. Minorities fall farther behind at each step of the educational ladder. African Americans earn bachelor's degrees at half the rate of white non-Hispanics, and Hispanics at an even lower rate. By 2020, minority populations will grow to half of high-school-age youth. Their educational achievement must rise to a level comparable to white non-Hispanics.

Despite current aggressive school reform, substantial numbers of young Americans will reach adulthood underprepared for employment in the information-rich 21st century. For these students, community college remedial education is a critical bridge to life success. Remedial education pays dividends. Each year more than half a million people enroll in remedial programs and gain the skills to become positive contributors to society. These students find high-skill employment. At a cost of only 1 percent of U.S. higher education expenditures, remedial education is the nation's most cost-effective educational program.

Underprepared Students

Despite their many achievements, community colleges can do better. Although some have exceptional remedial education programs, as a group community colleges fall short. They ignore what is known about underprepared student learning. They offer courses in easy-to-organize traditional classroom arrangements and rely too much on underpaid part-time instructors. Remedial education programs often survive on marginal budgets.

Legislators fail to see the value of remedial education and batter the programs during annual budget hearings. Some, believing that public schools have failed, respond by limiting community college remedial education programs. Consequently, they punish the young people that high schools have failed by denying them opportunities for completing their education. Each student who is denied opportunity for educational growth is a national resource lost. In the information age, we cannot have too many well-educated people.

The new economy offers our nation promise and peril. Tomorrow's workplace—information intense and technologically advanced—ensures an abundance of better jobs that could bring prosperity to more Americans. For this to be achieved, we must be fully committed to a fundamental value: belief in the importance of every person and full development of the talents of all our citizens. The nation can remain strong only if all Americans share in prosperity.

Community college remedial education is essential to developing a workforce for the information age. Each year remedial education salvages the lives of thousands of young people, and it deserves aggressive support from public decision-makers and colleges. America has no one to waste.

The Study

Twenty-five community colleges were selected to participate in the study, based on region, type of institution (urban, rural, and other), and the concentration of each type of institution in various regions. Research questions were identified through a poll of public decision-makers, community college leaders, and representatives of participating colleges.

The colleges used a random process to select 1,520 people who began remedial education in 1990, 592 of whom completed their remedial program successfully. The colleges collected data from student records and followed up with interviews of the successful cohort. With the help of a search firm, 71 percent of the successful students were contacted. Interviews yielded additional information about further education, employment, family, and facts about postremedial life. A criminal justice search was also conducted on the entire study cohort. These data were the basis for this first comprehensive national study on community college remedial education students.

In order to set the educational and social context for the provision of community college remedial education, research papers were commissioned on the current knowledge of community college remedial education and the societal context in which colleges provide remedial programs. The papers discussed demographics; poverty; immigration; the new American family; school reform; and business, industry, and work. Information drawn from these papers is presented in chapter 1.

The study also addressed a burning issue in postsecondary education: Do we need, and will we continue to need, college-level remedial education? If the answer is no, all other concerns about remedial education are irrelevant. This issue is discussed in chapter 2. The chapter explores the changing demographics of the United States and addresses the reasons why the old view of remedial education as simply preparation for bachelor's degrees is no longer valid.

Chapter 3 presents key findings from the study, with supporting data. These findings underlie the recommendations in chapter 4, which are directed primarily to public decision-makers and community college leaders. Summary rationales accompany the recommendations.

Frequently, supporting data from other remedial studies is presented alongside the National Study findings. Unless otherwise indicated, the tables and figures presented in this report illustrate National Study results and are original to this work.

Community colleges often use the term *developmental* rather than *remedial* to refer to programs for underprepared students. There are other useful terms as well. The term *remedial* was selected for use in this study because it is familiar to and readily understood by legislators, who make up a primary audience for the study recommendations.

A report on the research design and procedures is available on the American Association of Community Colleges' Web site, www.aacc. nche.edu, and a more lengthy book including the full report of the study is forthcoming.

ACKNOWLEDGMENTS

This study would not have been possible without the considerable contributions of the 25 participating colleges. They used their own resources to collect data and to follow up with former students.

The following people contributed to the report through their research and support: Bryan Donnelly, Karen Paulson, Hunter R. Boylan, Heather M. Boylan, Philip R. Day, Laura Pincus, Clinton Cooper, Margaret Rivera, Gregory Kienzl, and Dee Patrick Saxon.

Special thanks are due to my wife, Arva Parks, to Laura Pincus, and Regina Dodd for their assistance in preparation of the report, and to Gregory Parks for assistance with graphics.

This report was made possible by the support of the Pew Charitable Trusts for the National Study of Community College Remedial Education.

1

COMMUNITY COLLEGE REMEDIAL EDUCATION TODAY

Community college remedial education programs have always been controversial. Despite being introduced to protect the quality of college credit courses and to ensure that students were academically prepared for these courses, they still are not universally valued or supported.

In the 1960s, the nation urgently strived for equality, and higher education responded by providing opportunities for people who previously had been excluded. As a result, remedial education programs became necessary. In the 1980s and 1990s, dissatisfaction with public schools escalated, and many legislators viewed college remedial education as a duplication of high school expenditures that, in addition, reduced college standards. Despite these concerns, college enrollments continued to grow and become more inclusive.

Expanding Opportunity

A half-century of increased access to college began with the passage of the GI Bill. Americans were committed to those who had "saved the world" by serving in the military during World War II. Congress gave returning GIs a valuable gift—the opportunity to attend college. The nation benefited almost immediately as a broadened base of educated workers fueled the transformation from wartime to peacetime industry. The United States triumphed; industries grew and created thousands of better jobs. Times were good in postwar years, but not for everyone. Minorities and others were left out.

In the 1960s, the public recognized that discriminatory injustices of the past needed to be corrected and that African Americans should be given equal opportunity to share in the benefits the United States had to offer.

College doors opened more widely, and more college facilities were built than in the previous two centuries. At the forefront of the expansion was the most American of institutions, the open-door multimission community college. Community colleges embodied a fundamental American value: belief in the worth and potential of every person.

Throughout the remainder of the century, the drive for expanded opportunity continued. Education leaders focused on opportunities not only for African Americans but for Hispanics and other underserved populations, including women, people with disabilities, and older people. As a result, higher education experienced a great democratization. As student bodies became more diverse, they included more students who were less prepared academically. Such diversity often disrupted traditional practices.

Reflecting public attitudes, community colleges embraced a completely open policy. They believed that students knew best what they could and could not do and that no barriers should restrict them. College credit was given for everything, including remedial course work. Colleges allowed students to enroll in any course, regardless of preparation. This openness, however, came with a price. Permitting individuals with wide ranges of skills to enroll in courses at random resulted in high failure and dropout rates, which lowered expectations. Faculty struggled to teach classes made up of students with widely varied academic skills. Academic performance suffered, and some students even graduated without college-certified competencies.

During much of the 1970s and early 1980s, a pitched battle was waged within community colleges over the introduction of mandatory testing and whether to count remedial education course credit toward graduation. Many minority advocates, concerned that minority students

Although a few community colleges still permit students to enroll in any course regardless of preparation, it has become increasingly clear that program quality in open-door colleges is dependent on remedial education programs. To succeed in college courses, underprepared students must raise their skills.

would be driven from colleges, vehemently opposed these changes. Although a few community colleges still permit students to enroll in any course regardless of preparation, it has become increasingly clear that program quality in open-door colleges is dependent on remedial education programs. To succeed in college courses, underprepared students must raise their skills.

Today, almost all community colleges offer remedial education courses, most in multiple levels. Mandatory entry testing is becoming more common, but nearly half of states still lack policies that require it. Even fewer states require mandatory placement.

The Debate over Remedial Education

For the past two decades, debate over remedial education has been intense. We celebrate the achievements of those who have succeeded through remedial education, and public attitudes strongly support open access to higher education. Legislators, on the other hand, often miss the essential connection between access and remedial education. They take out their frustrations with public school failures on community college remedial programs. They argue that if we allow students to retake basic skills courses, we encourage high school complacency and diminish college quality. Legislators assert that students are responsible for their own academic development and the underprepared should pay the consequences.

Those who support remedial education make compelling counterarguments. One cannot deny the national importance of a well-educated citizenry and workforce. Supporters highlight the low cost of college remedial education and the role of remedial education in sustaining high college standards. An obvious connection exists between open access to higher education and the American commitment to equality. Unfortunately, most of the debate on remedial education is based on anecdotes rather than facts.

Public Schools

Certainly some of the blame for student underpreparation rests with public schools. Almost everyone believes schools need dramatic improvement. A reform movement began in earnest in 1982, but for many years there appeared to be almost no progress. In the last several years, however, legislators and governors have shown new and impressive commitment to meaningful school reform. As a result, glimpses of positive change are appearing. There is widespread hope that these efforts will succeed, but striking circumstances exist that make meaningful progress increasingly difficult.

Policy

States have primary responsibility for educational programs—state legislatures allocate resources and make policy decisions. Because of this, remedial education rarely becomes a federal issue.

Twenty-seven of 44 states responding to a survey conducted as part of the study indicated that community colleges and universities were permitted to offer remedial education. Eleven of these states, however, designated community colleges as the primary providers of remedial education services. Of the 44 states, 24 had policies stipulating that remedial courses could neither be counted toward degree requirements nor applied as transfer credit to another institution. Although practices vary, awarding institutional credit (credit that is not included in degrees) is now the most common. In 1970, 32 percent of community colleges gave degree credit and 63 percent awarded institutional credit. By 1995, only 10 percent awarded degree credit and 81 percent awarded only institutional credit. During the same period, those giving no credit increased from 5 to 10 percent (Saxon and Boylan 2000).

Enrollment

Ninety five percent of community colleges offer remedial education courses, most in multiple ability levels. Forty-one percent of entering community college students and 29 percent of all entering college students are underprepared in at least one of the basic skills (reading, writing, mathematics). Annually, more than one million underprepared students enter colleges and enroll in remedial programs. Of these students, 20 percent are deficient in reading, 25 percent are deficient in writing, and 34 percent are deficient in math (Saxon and Boylan 2000).

Fifty-four percent of remedial education students are under 24 years of age, 24 percent are between 25 and 34, and 17 percent are over 35. Female enrollment slightly exceeds male enrollment. Sixty-percent are white non-Hispanic, 23 percent are African American, and 12 percent are Hispanic. Fifty-four percent have an annual family income of less than $20,000.

Although the majority are white non-Hispanics, each minority group is overrepresented. Sixty-eight percent of remedial education students are enrolled full time, although most are working, many full time. Forty percent receive some form of financial aid (Saxon and Boylan 2000). The average credit load of remedial courses is approximately one-fourth of a full academic year. Despite the difficulties these students face, based on a number of studies, including this one, 40 to 50 percent of students are successful in their remedial education programs.

> *Forty-one percent of entering community college students and 29 percent of all entering college students are underprepared in at least one of the basic skills (reading, writing, mathematics).*

Programs

Even though community colleges advocate offering remedial education programs, these services frequently are given low priority. Programs are composed of courses often taught by poorly paid, part-time instructors.

To succeed, remedial education students need more than courses. They need personal support, which means more resources. Remedial education, however, is funded at a level equal to, or less than, standard community college work. Remedial programs typically are evaluated on the percentage of entrants who complete associate or baccalaureate degrees within some fixed time frame. This approach understates results and is inappropriate. It fails to take into account that most students attend part time and take a number of years to graduate. In addition, this system of evaluation looks at too narrow a definition of "success."

The following explores a changing demographic of the United States. It addresses the reasons why the old view of remedial education as simply preparation for bachelor's degrees is no longer valid.

2

WHY AMERICA DEPENDS ON COMMUNITY COLLEGE REMEDIAL EDUCATION

The United States is in a period of amazing change. We enjoy unprecedented prosperity and wondrous technology. Yet on the cusp of a new century, with all the opportunities and advancements, our nation still faces daunting challenges. To remain competitive in the global economy, we must reverse the growth of what seems to be a permanent underclass and develop a highly skilled workforce. The task of raising the competencies of our citizens falls on the educational system. Community colleges have a particularly important role. They educate the most deficient students and prepare them for employment and personal advancement.

Viewed from a societal perspective, it becomes clear that the United States needs all of its citizens prepared for the information-rich environment of the 21st century. Access to postsecondary education must, therefore, be a pillar of educational policy. The quality of college programs can be maintained only if remedial services are provided. Access and remedial education are inseparable.

Yet, the problem of underprepared citizens is not an educational issue alone. It is seated in and influenced by our rapidly changing society. Only in this context can the need for, and importance of, community college remedial education be understood. Demographic changes, continued poverty, and new family structures produce more underprepared stu-

> *The United States needs all of its citizens prepared for the information-rich environment of the 21st century. Access to post-secondary education must, therefore, be a pillar of educational policy.*

dents; public school failures result in competency deficiencies; the aging of the population shrinks the workforce; and ever-changing businesses and industries demand capable workers.

A Changing Nation

The United States of tomorrow will be older and far more diverse. Today, Hispanics number nearly 30 million and make up 11 percent of the population. With high birth rates and legal and illegal immigration, this percentage will increase. Hispanic Americans average 2.4 to 2.9 children per couple, compared with the white non-Hispanic average of just under 2 children per couple (Sivy 1997). In addition, the majority of today's immigrants are Hispanic, a trend that is expected to continue. From 1991 to 1994, immigrants from Latin America and the Caribbean numbered 2.3 million— 51.9 percent of immigrants to the United States (Fallon 1996).

According to Steven Holmes of the *New York Times*, Hispanics soon will overtake African Americans as the nation's largest minority population. By 2005, Hispanics will number more than 36 million, compared with a projected 35.5 million African Americans. By 2050, Hispanics are expected to make up almost one-quarter of the total population, or approximately 96 million people (Morganthau 1997). The growth is remarkable considering that in 1970 Hispanics accounted for just 9 million citizens, or roughly 4 percent of the national population (Friedman and Pollack 1996).

Immigrants and Hispanics will account for most of the population growth in the United States in the next 50 years. These populations are disproportionately underprepared for 21st-century employment, presenting a daunting task for education. Other minorities, including Asian American and African Americans, will have greater presence in the next decades. From 1991 to 1994, Asian immigrants

> *Immigrants and Hispanics will account for most of the population growth in the United States in the next 50 years. These populations are disproportionately underprepared for 21st-century employment, presenting a daunting task for education.*

composed nearly 30 percent of total immigration (Fallon 1996). By 2050, their population will increase by more than 220 percent, growing from nearly 10 million to more than 32 million. African Americans, in addition, will nearly double in population, increasing from more than 32 million to 53 million. Table 2.1 illustrates the projected population growth by race and ethnicity through the year 2050.

TABLE 2.1 POPULATION TRENDS (IN THOUSANDS)

ETHNICITY	1998	2010	2020	2030	2040	2050
White (non-Hispanic)	195,786	202,390	207,393	209,998	209,621	207,901
	72.5%	68.0%	64.3%	60.5%	56.7%	52.8%
Black (non-Hispanic)	32,789	37,466	41,538	45,448	49,379	53,555
	12.1%	12.6%	12.9%	13.1%	13.3%	13.6%
Hispanic Origin (any race)	29,566	41,139	52,652	65,570	80,164	96,508
	11.0%	13.8%	16.3%	18.9%	21.7%	24.5%
American Indian, Eskimo, and Aleut (non-Hispanic)	2,005	2,320	2,601	2,891	3,203	3,534
	.7%	.8%	.8%	.8%	.9%	.9%
Asian, Pacific Islander (non-Hispanic)	9,856	14,402	18,557	22,993	27,614	32,432
	3.7%	4.8%	5.7%	6.6%	7.5%	8.2%

Source: U.S. Bureau of the Census 1999.

A Majority Minority Nation

These projections point to a profound change in the nation's portrait. By the year 2050, the United States will be almost a "majority minority" country. Non-Hispanic whites will make up 53 percent of the population, down from nearly 75 percent today. The shift is more dramatic when considering the nation's youth. Before the year 2020, half of American youth will be minority (Hodgkinson 1997). The population will not be dominated by any one group but instead will be made up of clusters of different ethnicities and races. The changes, according to Ben Wattenberg of the American

Enterprise Institute, will make the United States "the first universal nation in human history" (Friedman and Pollack 1996, 16).

Multiethnicity

Accurately describing the demographics of the future becomes a tricky proposition. The term *Hispanic*, for example, invented for the 1980 census in an attempt to classify the large numbers of people from South and Central America, today describes such diverse populations as Cubans in Florida, Mexicans in California and Texas, and Puerto Ricans in New York (Hodgkinson 1998). Each group enjoys its own ethnic traditions, asserts its own cultural identity, and brings its own set of needs into classrooms. They are not homogeneous. As journalist Jack White explains, "The color line once drawn between blacks and whites—or more precisely between whites and nonwhites—is breaking into a polygon of dueling ethnicities, each fighting for its place in the sun" (1997, 33).

The census projections in table 2.1 tell only half the story. They characterize the country with broadly painted strokes that cannot fit into all of the nation's contours. They hint at America's changing face. The projections may understate the transformation to come. The 1990 census undercounted the population by 4.7 million people, with minorities a disproportionate part of that number. Even with inexact categories and imprecise counts, the trend is clear: In the next century, the image of the United States as a melting pot will become more accurate and appropriate.

Quite clearly, the nation's future will depend on our ability to improve all facets of life for a new nonwhite majority.

The Gray Wave

Ethnicity is not the only demographic force at work. The graying of America will be equally profound. The baby boomer generation, 76 million citizens born between the end of World War II and 1964, will begin to age and retire (Peterson 1996). They will trade in their "boomer" label for a new one—the "gray generation." They will influence the future by sheer numbers as well as by culture. Today, nearly 1 in 5 Floridians are over the age of

65. But, this population cluster will no longer be unique to Florida. By 2025 at the latest, the proportion of all American residents who are elderly will be the same as the proportion in Florida today. By 2040, 1 in 4 Americans may be over 65. Author Peter G. Peterson explains, "America in effect will become a nation of Floridas—and then keep aging" (1996, 56).

> *As much of the U.S. population ages and the workforce shrinks, it will be up to the education system to ensure that all Americans in their prime work years are prepared for employment. We will need everyone.*

By 2030, the elderly will account for 20 percent of the total population, increasing from 13 percent today. The number of people in the workforce will remain at 160 million, and the ratio of workers to the elderly will be halved. As much of the U.S. population ages and the workforce shrinks, it will be up to the education system to ensure that all Americans in their prime work years are prepared for employment. We will need everyone.

An examination of the Social Security system shows one important result. When the system began, there were 17 to 20 workers paying into the system for each retired worker receiving benefits. By 1960, the ratio had fallen to 5 workers for each retiree. Today it is 3.4 to 1, and by 2020, it is predicted that there will only be 2 workers for each retiree.

TABLE 2.2 NUMBER OF OLDER AMERICANS AND AMERICANS IN THEIR PRIME WORK YEARS (IN MILLIONS)

Americans	1995	2010	2030
Over 65 Years of Age	33.5	39.4	69.3
Prime Work Years	160.0	160.0	160.0

Source: Preston 1999.

A New Paradigm

Against the backdrop of aging baby boomers is a scientific community with unlimited potential. Medical advancements already prolong life and enhance its quality. Although it is difficult to predict what science will be able to do in the next century, most experts believe that medicine will redefine the aging process. Carl Haub of the Population Reference Bureau speculates that by 2050, the average life expectancy could reach 89, up from approximately 76 in 1995 (Peyser 1999). Census information predicts that by 2050, whites will live to age 84, Hispanics to 87, African Americans to 74, Asians to 86, and Native Americans to 82 (Morganthau 1997). The number of "young old" (65 to 69) will roughly double over the next half-century. The number of "old old" (85 and over) will triple or quadruple (Peterson 1996). In fact, by 2050 more than 18 million Americans will be over 85 (Morganthau 1997). The median age will rise from 35.2 to 38.1. Demographer James Vaupel concludes that we are now on the threshold of a "new paradigm of aging" in which the average life expectancy could reach 100 or more (Peterson 1996, 58).

With fewer members of the population in their prime work years, it will be increasingly important that all of our youth gain the high competencies necessary for employment. We will need everyone in their prime work years participating in the workforce and being sufficiently productive to support the growing elderly population.

Poverty

Despite our current prosperity, the United States continues to have a persistent underclass. For those who have not experienced it, it is hard to envision the difficulties of growing up in poverty surrounded by a sea of prosperity. Children growing up in poverty frequently do not have proper medical care; are often undernourished; and face challenges of life that frequently seem insurmountable, with violence, abuse, sexual assault, drugs, and often adult responsibilities for younger children, as a part of life. Poverty has the highest correlation with educational underpreparation at every level, from preschool to graduate school. The United States has the highest rate of poverty of all developed nations.

How can we explain poverty's impact? Why are minorities such a larger proportion of our nation's poor? The answer rests with fundamental quality-of-life issues. Jason DeParle of the *New York Times* explains:

> On average, [minorities have had] less education, lower incomes, and more children. They [are] less likely to have ever been married, a statistic that predicts lower rates of child support and lessened chances of leaving the rolls through subsequent marriage. . . . Minority recipients [are] much more likely to live in poor, central city neighborhoods, far from the job growth that rings many cities. (27 July 1998)

Ample evidence indicates that family income affects children's education. In 1999, Florida introduced a plan to give grades to public schools based on student performance on standardized tests. Walter R. Tschinkel, writing for the *Tallahassee Democrat*, found that 80 percent of the school grades could be attributed to the level of poverty among that school's students. Tschinkel writes, "Because standardized test performance is reliably predicted by poverty, the poverty-level of a school is by far the strongest predictor of the school's grade" (17 February 2000).

Poverty has the highest correlation with educational underpreparation at every level, from preschool to graduate school. The United States has the highest rate of poverty of all developed nations.

Poor children begin their lives with every conceivable disadvantage: poor parental care, lack of early education, inadequate healthcare, and unstimulating household environments. One result is lower learning achievement when compared with children from higher income families. They simply are not on an even playing field. Table 2.3 shows the meager prospects of poor youth obtaining a bachelor's degree.

TABLE 2.3 COLLEGE GRADUATES:
HIGH INCOME VERSUS LOW INCOME

College Graduates by Age 24	Percentage
Young People from High-Income Families	48%
Young People from Low-Income Families	7%

Source: Education Trust 1998.

Stories of the plight of people give poverty a face. But harsh statistics truly capture the scope of the crisis. In 1997, the U.S. poverty rate was 13.3 percent, with 35.6 million poor citizens. The poverty threshold for a family of four was $16,400 and for a family of three, $12,802. The number of poor was 3.2 million more than the 1989 level of 32.4 million. At the same time, the U.S. economy boomed and median household income reached a high of $37,005 (Weinberg 1998).

More than three decades after President Lyndon B. Johnson waged his War on Poverty, countless Americans are still left behind, especially minority citizens. African American and Hispanic welfare recipients outnumber whites by almost 2 to 1. By early 1997, African Americans accounted for 37 percent of the nation's welfare caseload, though they made up just 13 percent of the general population. Hispanics accounted for 22 percent (up from 12 percent in 1983), though they amounted to just 11 percent of the population. By contrast, whites were 35 percent of the welfare rolls, though they represented 73 percent of the population.

Children at Risk

In the new American family, there is simply less time for children. Families are more diverse and increasingly do not involve a full-time father. In 1963, 77 percent of white children, 65 percent of Hispanic children, and 36 percent of African American children lived in a two-parent family. By 1991, only half of U.S. children and teens lived in a traditional nuclear family. Fifty percent of white children live with a divorced mother; 54 percent of African American children and 33 percent of Hispanic children have mothers who have never been married. More children are born to unmarried women—33 percent in 1994—compared with 5 percent in 1960. Even two-parent households spend less family time together. Approximately 70 percent of mothers with children are working, and children are often shuttled between daycare centers, baby sitters, and extended family members.

Three problems that have a major impact on a child's learning abilities include insufficient parenting, poor prenatal care, and inadequate healthcare. All of these are exacerbated by the changes in family structure. In 1994, the number of children living in poverty reached more than 15.3 million—up from 10.2 million just two decades earlier (Hodgkinson 1997; Lichter 1997). The people most affected by poverty are the children. According to the Annie C. Casey Foundation's 1996 *Kids County Data Sheet*, in the United States, nearly 25 percent of children under the age of six live in poverty. Although children made up only 27 percent of the U.S. population, they accounted for 40 percent of all poor people (Lichter 1997).

The people most affected by poverty are the children. According to the Annie C. Casey Foundation's 1996 Kids County Data Sheet, in the United States, nearly 25 percent of children under the age of six live in poverty.

Child poverty is also divided along racial and ethnic lines. Table 2.4 examines the high poverty rate of African American and Hispanic children in comparison with white children (Lichter 1997).

Even more troubling, the Columbia University National Center for Children in Poverty reports that 30 percent of young African American children (1.9 million) live in families that have incomes below half of the federal poverty threshold. This "extreme poverty" applies to only 6 percent of white children (2.2 million) (*Jet* 1996, 32).

TABLE 2.4 POVERTY AMONG U.S. CHILDREN: 1994

Ethnicity	Percentage Living in Poverty
Total Children	21.8%
White Children	16.9%
African American Children	43.8%
Hispanic Children	41.5%

Source: Lichter 1997.

The Working Poor

Policymakers who look at these statistics typically might see employment as a remedy. However, the reality is that working is not always a ticket out of poverty. People need good jobs—that is, jobs with a living wage. In 1960, a young adult with a full-time minimum-wage job could keep a family of three out of poverty. In 1994, such a person would make only 70 percent of the amount needed to keep a family out of poverty (Hodgkinson 1997). This creates a new category of Americans—the working poor. In 1994, the number of children of the working poor rose to 5.6 million from 3.4 million two decades ago—a 65 percent increase ("Social Science and the Citizen" 1996). These children are even more at risk than children on welfare because they are not eligible for Medicaid, and their mothers must pay for childcare services (Hill 1998).

Beyond the Statistics

The numbers reveal a nation of haves and have-nots. Millions of Americans, including a disproportionate number of minorities and children, live below the poverty line.

The *Monthly Labor Review* provides a broader perspective of the poor. In a comprehensive May 1996 article, nine academics analyzed surveys on housing, consumer expenditures, population, demographics, health, crime, and income to paint a bleak picture of living conditions. The poor, for example, are five times more likely to be evicted from their housing than economically stable citizens. They have less access to basic household needs.

The poor are twice as likely as nonpoor to be victims of violent crimes, and those in single-parent poor households are three times more likely. Poor mothers experience a higher rate of infant mortality, receive less prenatal care, and are less likely to have medical insurance (Federman et al. 1996).

Growing Up Poor

Clearly, the United States is not doing enough to combat poverty. But what does growing up poor in our nation really mean? What impact does economics have on childhood, education, and life choices? What is most likely to happen to the 15 million poor children as they reach maturity?

Poor and nonpoor mothers experience pregnancy and motherhood quite differently. The Centers for Disease Control and Prevention define inadequate prenatal care as lack of doctor visits in the first trimester. Forty-three percent of poor mothers and 49 percent of poor, single mothers had no prenatal care, compared with only 16 percent of nonpoor mothers (Federman et al. 1996). Yet, scientists know that early intervention can prevent birth defects such as Down syndrome and other developmental and physical impairments. Even before they are born, poor children could be steps behind.

Early years are crucial to the development of a human being. Demographer Harold L. Hodgkinson explains that "new brain research has shown that half of what a person learns over a lifetime is learned before kindergarten" (1999, 3). Brain development research also shows that "wiring of neurons occurs after birth and that experience during infancy and early childhood plays a critical role in defining an individual's capacity to learn. The child's brain and central nervous system develop rapidly during the first three years of life in response to parental attention and stimulation, such as talking, seeing, and playing. Infants who live without talking, playing, and interacting suffer a permanent loss of learning capacity." This loss occurs more frequently in single-parent families or families who have less time to spend with their children. The decline of the traditional family and the rising percentage of children born into poverty increase the number of persons who will enter school unprepared and who will have inadequate parental support. More of these individuals will reach adulthood educationally underprepared and will probably need community college remedial education at some point in their lives.

BUSINESS/INDUSTRY AND WORK

The 20th century has been the setting for continuous changes in the U.S. labor force. The nature of business and industry evolved through the Industrial Revolution and post–World War II peacetime conversion of wartime industries. The information age revolution has escalated changes to lightning speed. These changes constantly reshape the skills necessary for meaningful employment.

The U.S. Workforce in the 20th Century

In 1900, the United States supported and was maintained by predominantly goods-producing industries (figure 2.1), which employed two-thirds of American workers. Agriculture, forestry, and fisheries employed 37.6 percent; manufacturing and hand trades 21.8 percent; construction 5.7 percent; and mining 2.6 percent.

The 1990 census indicates that the percentage of workers employed in goods-producing industries had seriously dwindled to little more than one-quarter of the American workforce (27.8 percent). The industries with the most marked decline were agriculture, forestry, and fisheries, which were down from 37.6 percent in 1900 to a mere 2.7 percent by 1990. Winners in the non-goods-producing sector were the trade industry, up from 8.2 percent to 20.7 percent, and service (combined categories) industries, which increased from 13.3 percent of employment to 33.1 percent.

As we enter the 21st century, the educational system has fallen behind and is no longer keeping pace with industry's information explosion.

Through most of the 20th century, more people completed higher levels of education, keeping pace with changes in industry. As industries changed, occupations did as well. From 1900 to 1990, white-collar workers increased from 17.6 percent to 58.2 percent of the employed population. As we enter the 21st century,

FIGURE 2.1 INDUSTRIAL TRENDS OF THE 20TH CENTURY

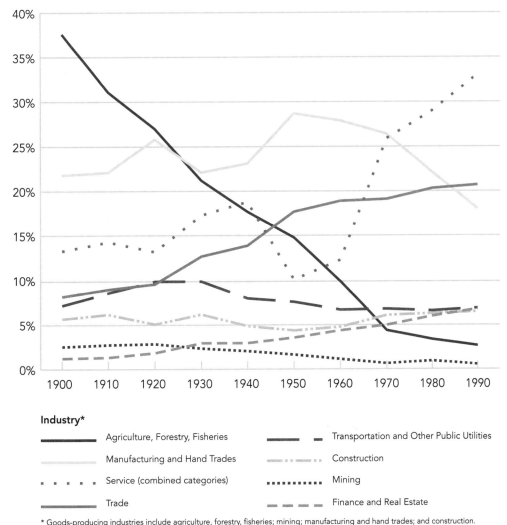

Industry*

——————— Agriculture, Forestry, Fisheries   — — — Transportation and Other Public Utilities

——————— Manufacturing and Hand Trades   — · · — Construction

· · · · · Service (combined categories)   · · · · · · · · · · Mining

——————— Trade   – – – – Finance and Real Estate

* Goods-producing industries include agriculture, forestry, fisheries; mining; manufacturing and hand trades; and construction. Non-goods-producing industries (service industries) include transportation and other public utilities; trade; finance and real estate, service (combined categories); and government not elsewhere classified.

Source: U.S. Bureau of Labor Statistics Series D 127-141, Series D 152-166, and Series D 167-181; U.S. Bureau of the Census 1975 and 1997.

the educational system has fallen behind and is no longer keeping pace with industry's information explosion.

What were some of the factors that contributed to the conversion of the United States from a primarily agricultural and goods-producing economy to a service- and trade-oriented economy? First, the Industrial Revolution made an agrarian workforce obsolete as mechanization replaced agricultural workers and made manufacturing preeminent in urban areas (Blau and Ferber 1986; Carnevale 1996; Durand 1968; Gordon, Edwards, and Reich 1982; Marshall and Tucker 1992). Second, World War II precipitated not only the influx of women into the workforce but also an increase in the number of white-collar workers traced to GI Bill–college graduates (Blau and Ferber 1986; Durand 1968; Gordon, Edwards, and Reich 1982). Change in the labor force caused by the Industrial Revolution and World War II precipitated changes in the skill level and education necessary for employment in the new economy.

As the 21st Century Begins

In the last decades of the 20th century, a new phenomenon shaped the workplace—the primary currency for employment became advanced education. In the 1950s, most (60 percent) available jobs required only unskilled labor, while some required basic information skills (20 percent), and some required professional training (20 percent). By the 1990s, the balance shifted dramatically, with the demand for unskilled workers declining steeply (35 percent), and the demand for skilled workers increasing just as rapidly (45 percent), a trend that is continuing at the same rate. Today, most (65 percent) jobs require skilled or professionally trained (20 percent) workers, with relatively few (15 percent) jobs requiring unskilled labor, a shift that represents a complete realignment of the need for skilled and unskilled workers during the past half-century. And in the next six years, nearly 80 percent of new jobs will require advanced or superior skills (Carnevale and Desrochers 1999).

As a direct result of the dynamic change in job requirements, the need for postsecondary education and training has climbed dramatically. Hickman and Quinley identified new skill sets by reviewing literature on workforce education and training, noting that today computer literacy is the top priority of employers, with more than 80 percent of the jobs requiring at least some facility with technology (1997). In fact, 51 percent of today's workforce is expected to use a computer on a daily basis for mathematics (65 percent), reading (55 percent), and writing (30 percent) tasks. This represents double the usage required a decade earlier. Also included among the top six skills are cognitive and noncognitive abilities associated with the workforce of the future. Interpersonal and team skills (79 percent), critical thinking skills (75 percent), personal and work ethic skills (67 percent), leadership and supervisory skills (67 percent), and quality-improvement skills (66 percent) are the other five top priorities of today's employers.

The workforce of the 21st century will be quite different from that of the 20th century—the result of revolution and evolution. Revolutionary changes will result from the effects of increasing globalization and proliferating technology. Evolutionary changes will occur as existing jobs require markedly different skill sets. A given job title will need different behaviors and skills from those that employees may currently possess. Recently, 56 percent of corporations surveyed indicated they had restructured nonmanagerial jobs largely around new technology, while only 5 percent decreased required skill levels (U. S. Department of Commerce et al. 1999; Soul 1998). In addition, computer technology is revolutionizing not only how processes are carried out but also what organizational structures maximize the effectiveness of integrating technology. Workers must be empowered to use computers to everyone's best advantage (Carnevale 1996). Simple jobs are becoming high performance, thus requiring workers to reason through complex processes rather than follow rote behavioral instructions for how to complete discrete steps of larger processes.

The Ford Motor Company began the new millennium with a dramatic demonstration of the importance of an information-competent workforce by buying computers for all of its 300,000 employees. A report of the National Alliance of Business states that "with the explosion of technology in the workplace, skill-level requirements are being ratcheted up by employers. Inventory, sales marketing, expense analysis, communications, and corresponding are being done faster, better, and cheaper and with greater efficiency in the workplace" (Greenberg 1997, 6).

With turbulent years of reorganization, companies have raised skill requirements in order to hire employees with the competencies they need to be more competitive. More highly skilled workers have replaced employees with outdated skills. Job elimination and downsizing have declined to their lowest levels in a decade as companies prepare for increased productivity and profitability. Eric Greenberg, director of management studies for the American Management Association, states,

TABLE 2.5 SUMMARY OF 21ST-CENTURY BASIC JOB SKILLS

Attitudes and Personal Characteristics

> Adaptability, flexibility, resiliency, and ability to accept ambiguity
> Common sense and ability to anticipate downstream consequences
> Creativity
> Empathy
> Positive attitude, good work ethic, and ability to self-manage
> Reliability and dependability
> Responsibility, honesty, and integrity

Essential Skills

> Computers for simple tasks (word processing)
> Interpersonal skills, team skills
> Numeracy and computation skills at a ninth-grade level, including basic money skills
> Reading at a ninth-grade level
> Speaking and listening
> Writing

Integrative and Applied Skills

> Application of technology to tasks
> Critical thinking
> Customer contact skills
> Information use skills
> Presentation skills
> Problem recognition/definition and solution formulation
> Reasoning

Premium Skills

> Ability to understand organizational and contextual issues (legal, environmental)
> Basic resource management, budgets
> Ethics
> Foreign language fluency
> Globalism, internationalism skills
> Multicultural-competence skills
> Negotiation skills
> Project management and supervision
> Systems thinking

"The same forces that were costing jobs in the early years, such as restructuring, reengineering, and automation are now creating jobs that demand high skill levels. People going out the door don't have them, the people coming in do" (1997). Twenty-first century job skills are more complex and require more education (table 2.5).

The problem of citizens underprepared for employment in the new economy is already becoming evident. Since 1990, companies have been allowed to recruit foreign-born, highly skilled workers through the HI-B visa program. Until 1997, the quota was not used. But pressed by industry, Congress temporarily expanded the program in 1998, increasing the number of six-year visas from 65,000 to 115,000 per year. The high-tech industry reached the quota in 2000, and, citing a lack of highly skilled Americans, is now pushing Congress for an expansion to 200,000 (*Miami Herald*, 4 February 2000, 4C).

Business and industry estimate that 80 percent of the 21st-century workforce will need some postsecondary education. In addition, workers will need higher-order information competencies as a base for lifelong education. The United States has a long way to go to develop the broadly based, highly skilled workforce needed in a global economy. Business and industry will use the least costly method to achieve its goals. Already, manufacturing is moving from the United States to less-developed nations where wages are lower—a trend that will continue. Sustaining the country's future will depend on leading and developing knowledge industries based on highly skilled and more productive workers. Brain power and technology can multiply individual productivity, thus compensating for higher wages and helping the U.S. retain global competitiveness.

Experts believe that countries that remain competitive in the 21st century will be those with the highest overall literacy and educational achievement levels, such as Germany and Japan, which have a strong "bottom third." This should be a compelling wake-up call. Because of demographic shifts, the task of raising the bottom third in the United States, will become considerably more difficult.

SCHOOL REFORM

Americans generally agree that the results of the public school system are unsatisfactory. This problem sparked a school-reform movement that gained momentum through the last two decades of the 20th century but produced limited improvements. The program for better-prepared students improved, but the percentage of students who finished high school underprepared varied little.

Recently, governors and state legislators have vigorously pursued more improvements, and these efforts are producing some positive signs. Most encouraging is an increase during the past decade (from 12.7 to 46.8) in the percentage of students taking the "new basic" curriculum, a core of academic courses. But all is not well. The tracking system in U.S. high schools still has a stronghold. Schools systematically place more than half of their students in general and vocational tracks that do not adequately prepare them for an information-rich environment. The percentage of students receiving regular high school diplomas has declined. Nine percent are now receiving certificates of attendance, and most disturbing, a higher percentage is graduating with either a general equivalency diploma (GED) or a similar alternate diploma.

The basic tenet of all reform is to ensure that all students develop strong academic/information competencies. The school reform efforts are laudable and necessary. Yet, too much should not be expected, as the challenges facing public education are tremendous and promise to become even more difficult.

The Education Dilemma

Demographic realities—particularly growing diversity—will have a profound impact on the educational system. Today, children come to classrooms with different diets, different religions, different individual and group loyalties, different music, and different languages. Therefore, schools become more like a patchwork of cultures than a common community. Los Angeles Hollywood High School, for example, once a white, non-Hispanic school of well-off students, now houses a student body that speaks 57 languages; for

92 percent, English is a second language. How do children learn, and how do faculty teach, without a common culture or language?

Future students will be problematic for an even more profound reason—lack of academic skill. Teachers will struggle not only with student diversity but with students' poor language skills and lack of educational attainment. Minority populations increasingly lag academically. Only 61 percent of Hispanics graduate from high school with a regular high school diploma, and only 10 percent earn baccalaureate degrees. Among African Americans, 86 percent graduate from high school and 15 percent earn baccalaureate degrees. How successful will we be in developing a highly skilled workforce when 25 percent of our young people are Hispanic?

The difficulty of the task facing American education is depicted in figure 2.2. The goal for public education should be to graduate 80 percent of students with college-entry skills. We are a long way from that goal. Only 67 percent of young Americans are earning standard high school diplomas, and only 42 percent of those are graduating with college-entry skills. High school graduation standards are at a level lower than college-entry skills.

FIGURE 2.2 K–12 TRENDS AFFECTING PERCENTAGE OF STUDENTS GRADUATING FROM HIGH SCHOOL WITH OR WITHOUT COLLEGE-ENTRY SKILLS

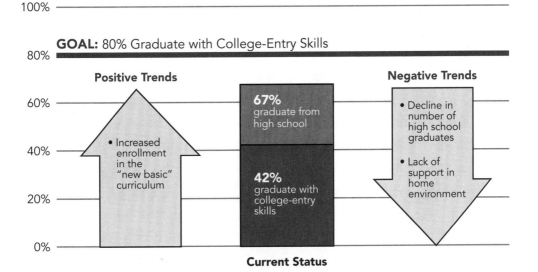

The most difficult impediment to educational improvement is the growth of populations that are underprepared, which results in more youngsters lacking school-readiness skills, and an increase in the number of children growing up without needed support in their home environment. It is safe to assume that despite school-reform gains, public schools will not reach the 80 percent goal. In fact, it will take a strong effort not to lose ground.

Although some high school dropouts later earn GEDs, the percentage of students who graduate from high school with a standard diploma has declined from 73 percent in 1983 to 67 percent in 1997. In 1997 and 1998, of 3.6 million ninth graders, 2.4 million became regular high school graduates and 1.2 million dropped out. This waste of human resources is destructive to the nation.

Figure 2.3 shows the critical lack of preparedness among youth in the United States and displays the progression of students from ninth grade through college/workforce entry and how they match with 21st-century job readiness. The figure portrays the imposing information-competency gap facing the United States.

Of all students who enter ninth grade, 84 percent graduate from high school. This percentage includes 16 percent who earn a GED or other alternate diploma by age 24. Fifty-nine percent of those who entered ninth grade eventually enroll in college, but only 42 percent are actually prepared for college-level work.

In the 21st century, 80 percent of new jobs will require some postsecondary education, while 20 percent will be unskilled jobs. About 42 percent of postsecondary students are prepared for skilled positions, indicating that 38 percent of the new jobs will go unfilled. Of the students who originally entered ninth grade, 58 percent are prepared only for unskilled jobs. More than a third of additional young Americans will require postsecondary information skill development, including remedial education, to be employable in the 21st century.

Figure 2.4 depicts the same progression through the educational system as that shown in figure 2.3, but with a forecasted population for 2020—when 50 percent of American youth will be nonwhite—and an assumption that

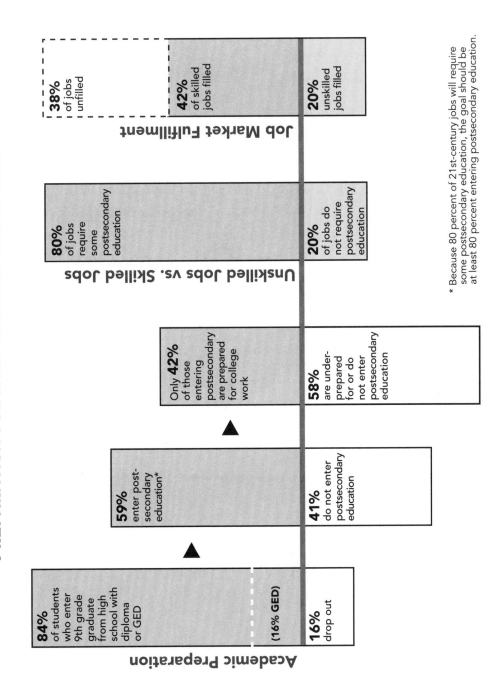

FIGURE 2.3 EDUCATIONAL PROGRESSION OF YOUNG AMERICANS IN PREPARATION FOR 21ST-CENTURY EMPLOYMENT

Academic Preparation

84% of students who enter 9th grade graduate from high school with diploma or GED

(16% GED)

16% drop out

59% enter post-secondary education*

41% do not enter postsecondary education

Only **42%** of those entering postsecondary are prepared for college work

58% are under-prepared for or do not enter postsecondary education

Unskilled Jobs vs. Skilled Jobs

80% of jobs require some postsecondary education

20% of jobs do not require postsecondary education

Job Market Fulfillment

38% of jobs unfilled

42% of skilled jobs filled

20% unskilled jobs filled

* Because 80 percent of 21st-century jobs will require some postsecondary education, the goal should be at least 80 percent entering postsecondary education.

Substantial numbers of people will reach adulthood without the skills necessary for employment in the information age. Effective community college remedial education must be there for these individuals. It is their lifeline to the future.

there has been no educational progress. A devastating picture results. Decline from an already poor situation is evident. High school graduates, including those with GEDs, decline from 84 to 82 percent, those entering college decline from 59 percent to 51 percent, and those prepared for college or 21st-century employment decline from 42 percent to 33 percent. Sixty-seven percent would be prepared only for 20 percent of the jobs.

In preparing American youth for life in the 21st century, our educational system is underperforming drastically. Progress is expected through educational reform efforts, but the task is overwhelming. The data indicate that substantial numbers of people will reach adulthood without the skills necessary for employment in the information age. Effective community college remedial education must be there for these individuals. It is their lifeline to the future.

FIGURE 2.4 PREDICTED EDUCATIONAL PROGRESSION OF 2020 YOUNG AMERICANS IN PREPARATION FOR 21ST-CENTURY EMPLOYMENT

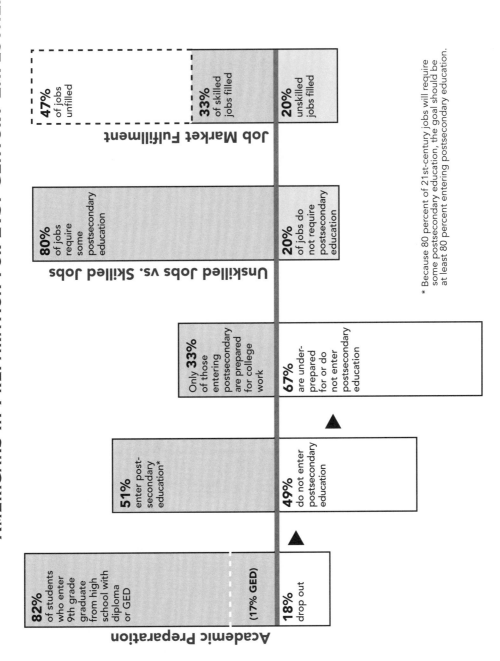

Academic Preparation

82% of students who enter 9th grade graduate from high school with diploma or GED

(17% GED)

18% drop out

51% enter post-secondary education*

49% do not enter postsecondary education

Only **33%** of those entering postsecondary are prepared for college work

67% are under-prepared for or do not enter postsecondary education

Unskilled Jobs vs. Skilled Jobs

80% of jobs require some postsecondary education

20% of jobs do not require postsecondary education

Job Market Fulfillment

47% of jobs unfilled

33% of skilled jobs filled

20% unskilled jobs filled

* Because 80 percent of 21st-century jobs will require some postsecondary education, the goal should be at least 80 percent entering postsecondary education.

3
FINDINGS

This chapter presents the major findings of the National Study of Community College Remedial Education. The findings are followed by brief explanations or pertinent related information.

Finding 1. Nearly half of community college remedial education students successfully complete their program.

In this study, 43 percent of community college remedial education students successfully completed their program. Other studies have shown similar results, with success rates between 40 and 50 percent.

The ethnic makeup of those who were successfully remediated was remarkably similar to the entire remedial education cohort.

Finding 2. Successfully remediated students perform well in standard college work.

Studies show that academic performance of successful remedial education students is almost identical to that of students who enter community college academically prepared. Some research has shown even better performance, particularly in retention. A study of Florida Community Colleges showed that a third of associate degree graduates had enrolled in remedial courses. With regard to the potential of remedial education students, this finding is encouraging.

Like other studies, this one showed good performance in standard college courses by successful remedial education students. These students passed 88 percent of standard college English classes and 82 percent of standard college mathematics classes.

Finding 3. Most successful remedial education students gravitate to occupational programs or direct employment.

Today, remedial programs are designed primarily to prepare students for bachelor's degrees. In Florida, for example, remedial education courses are called college preparatory courses. This does not match with the actual paths taken by successful remedial education students, who proceed in greater numbers into occupational programs. Table 3.1 shows that 14 percent of these students earned academic associate degrees and 16.2 percent earned bachelor's degrees. The total who earned occupational degrees and certificates was 36.8 percent—15 percent occupational associate degrees and 21.8 percent certificates.

The statistics do not reflect students who enrolled in a selection of courses and gained the skills needed for employment without earning a degree or certificate. Many community college students follow this pattern, and it can be assumed that this was the case with a significant percentage of the study cohort. A greater percentage of the study cohort were prepared for employment than is indicated by degrees and certificates earned.

More than half of the study cohort earned more than 20 credits. These students continued their commitment to education nine years after remediation. Fifty percent of the students reported that they are either continuing

TABLE 3.1 DEGREES AND CERTIFICATES EARNED BY SUCCESSFUL REMEDIAL EDUCATION STUDENTS

Degree/Certificate	Percentage
Vocational Certificate	16.0%
Other Certificates	5.8%
Associate Degree–Occupational	15.0%
Total Occupational	**36.8%**
Associate Degree–Academic	14.0%
Bachelor's Degree	16.2%
Graduate Degree	3.7%

their education or are planning to do so. More than half of them report satisfaction with their careers and an intention to continue their current work or express a goal of advancement with their current employer.

Finding 4. Students who are successfully remediated become productively employed.

The study cohort of successful remedial education students includes teachers, lawyers, physicians, an assistant district attorney, and a television news anchor. The shining success, however, is the breadth of constructive life achievements of all of these students. Figure 3.1 shows that 98.5 percent of these individuals are employed; only 1.5 percent are out of the workforce. Nearly 90 percent are in jobs above the unskilled level, and 53.7 percent are in the fast-growing technical and midlevel, white-collar sectors. Only 1.5 percent had been convicted of a felony during the nine years following remedial education.

Data comparing a national cohort of similar demographics are strikingly different. That cohort shows 7 to 8 percent out of the workforce and approximately 8 percent convicted of a felony.

FIGURE 3.1 OCCUPATIONS OF SUCCESSFUL REMEDIAL EDUCATION STUDENTS

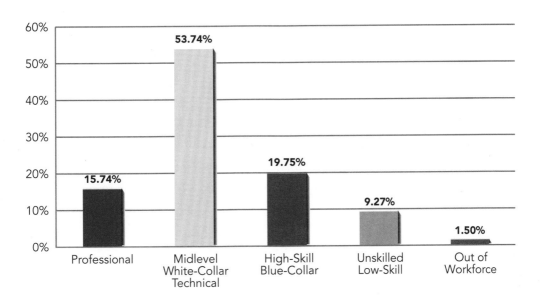

As a group, successful remedial education students become solid, contributing members of society. Investment in these individuals pays solid dividends.

Finding 5. Minorities have made progress but are far from achieving educational equality.

Minorities have made educational gains. From 1977 to 1997, the percentage of African American high school graduates enrolling in college increased from 49.6 percent to 59.6 percent, and the percentage of Hispanics increased from 46.9 percent to 55 percent. During the same period, however, the percentage of white non-Hispanic high school graduates enrolling in college also increased from 50.7 to 67.5 percent.

The statistics must be improved. African Americans and Hispanics lose ground at each step of the educational ladder—from high school graduation to college enrollment to bachelor's degrees earned.

African Americans make up 15.5 percent of 15- to 19-year-olds, but they earn only 10 percent of associate degrees and 8.6 percent of bachelor's degrees (table 3.3). Hispanics make up 14.4 percent of 15- to 19-year-olds, but they earn only 7.4 percent of associate degrees and 5.5 percent of bachelor's degrees. Most disturbing, 25.3 percent of Hispanics and 13.4 percent of African Americans drop out of high school. In contrast, 7.6 percent of white non-Hispanics drop out, and while they make up 70.1 percent of 15- to 19-year-olds, they earn 83.3 percent of associate degrees and 85.7 percent of bachelor's degrees (National Center for Education Statistics 1998).

Of special concern are African American men. Although they slightly outnumber African American women, only 32 percent of African American college graduates are men. They make up 7.8 percent of the age group but only 3.1 percent of college graduates. If equality had been achieved, 149,000 Hispanics would be college graduates rather than 58,288, and 163,000 African Americans would be graduates rather than 91,166. The number of African American men earning a bachelor's degree would rise from 32,832 to 82,000. The progressive dropoff in minority achievement is troublesome and unacceptable.

As we enter an information-intense work world, the staggering numbers of minorities failing to progress educationally bodes ill for the country. Achieving equality is fundamental to our values and essential to social and economic well-being. It would be destructive to our society if, because of lack of skills, large numbers of minorities were added to the underclass. In the future, minorities will make up half the workforce. They will need to develop strong skills to sustain U.S. business and industry.

TABLE 3.2 PERCENTAGE OF KINDERGARTNERS WHO ACHIEVE VARIOUS LEVELS OF EDUCATION

Ethnicity	Graduate from High School*	Some College	Bachelor's Degree
African American	86%	48%	15%
Hispanic	61%	31%	10%
White Non-Hispanic	93%	62%	29%

*Includes GED and other similar diplomas.
Source: Education Trust 1998.

TABLE 3.3 EDUCATIONAL PROGRESSION OF AFRICAN AMERICAN, HISPANIC, AND WHITE NON-HISPANIC STUDENTS

Ethnicity	Percentage of Population Aged 15–19	Percentage Who Graduate from High School	Percentage Who Enroll in College (Directly from H.S.)	Percentage Who Earn Associate Degrees	Percentage Who Earn Bachelor's Degrees
African American	15.5%	13.3%	11.6%	10.0%	8.6%
Hispanic	14.4%	11.3%	9.9%	7.4%	5.5%
White Non-Hispanic	70.1%	75.3%	78.4%	83.3%	85.7%

Source: National Center for Education Statistics 1998 and U.S. Bureau of the Census 1999.

Note: Because the reports include different groups, for example non-residents in college enrollment data, all data were restricted to African Americans, Hispanics, and white non-Hispanics. In each case the percentages were based on the data for only these three groups.

Finding 6. The demographics of seriously deficient students are dramatically different from other remedial education students.

Striking differences exist between seriously deficient students (those deficient in reading, writing, and mathematics and assigned to a lower-level remedial course in at least one area) and other remedial groups. The study shows that 56 percent of academically deficient students are white non-Hispanic, 23.4 percent are African American, and 12.5 percent are Hispanic. These data are consistent with other studies that report that the majority of underprepared students are white non-Hispanic, but minorities are overrepresented. Seriously deficient students were ethnically different from other deficient students. Three-quarters of these students were minorities—39.8 percent African American, 21.6 percent Hispanic, 8.8 percent Asian/Pacific Islander, 5.8 percent other—while 23.9 percent were white non-Hispanic (figure 3.2). Minority women were 51 percent of all seriously deficient students.

Minority underpreparation is clear when considering seriously deficient students. Only 5 percent of white non-Hispanics were seriously deficient, whereas about 20 percent of minority students were seriously deficient (figure 3.3). This finding has important implications. Because the majority of academically deficient students are white non-Hispanics, it has been thought that remedial education is not a special issue for minorities. The study shows that academic deficiencies affect minorities to a far greater extent than they do white non-Hispanics. For minorities, deficiencies produced through K–12 system inequities and disproportionate poverty are projected into college. America must vigorously address these circumstances.

FIGURE 3.2 PERCENTAGE OF STUDENTS ACADEMICALLY DEFICIENT AND SERIOUSLY DEFICIENT BY ETHNICITY

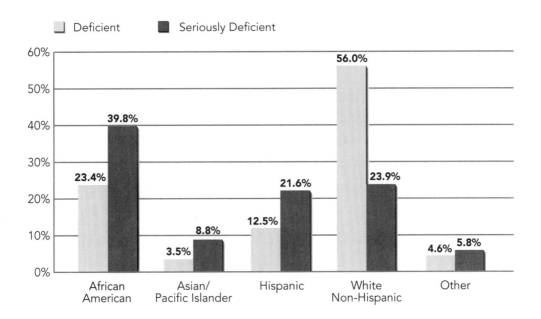

FIGURE 3.3 PERCENTAGE OF EACH ETHNIC GROUP SERIOUSLY DEFICIENT

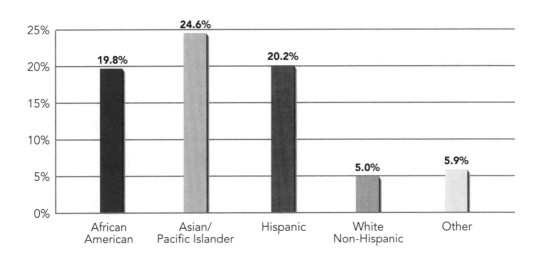

Finding 7. The success rate for seriously deficient students is unacceptably low.

The depth of academic underpreparation of deficient students is different from that of seriously deficient students. Deficient students had a 43 percent successful remediation rate, whereas only 20 percent of seriously deficient students were successful.

More than half of deficient students earned more than 20 college credits, while less than 5 percent of seriously deficient students earned more than 20 credits. Only 18 percent of deficient students enrolled in more than 12 remedial credits, while 45 percent of seriously deficient students did so.

The program for seriously deficient students is unsuccessful and should be revised. Remedial programs should be improved to provide skills that assist students in finding and maintaining employment and in improving quality of life. No ceilings should be imposed. Those completing program goals should be encouraged to proceed on to completion of regular remedial programs.

For these students, beginning college is fraught with difficulties, yet it is a major positive step in their lives. They deserve the best possible opportunities.

Finding 8. Community college remedial programs are not funded at a level necessary for successful results.

Academically underprepared students require more support and personal attention than other students. Most remedial education students have not had a good experience in high school, are returning to school well after high school completion, or both. A significant number of these students bring personal problems with them. They frequently have meager resources and have family and job obligations. All of this translates into a need for more interaction and support, and thus more cost.

Typically, states support remedial education courses at the same rate as basic academic programs—or less. In this study, only 2 of the 25 colleges reported above-average funding for these programs; 5 reported lower funding;

18 reported comparable funding. Public decision-makers are frequently upset by remedial program failure rates and demand improvement. This is only possible, however, when appropriate resources are provided.

In states that use program cost data for developing funding formulas, community colleges are their own worst enemies. They do not provide the necessary additional support; rather, they offer remedial courses using large numbers of inexpensive, part-time faculty. Expenditure-driven funding formulas produce low-cost projections, thus systematically underfunding the programs.

Finding 9. Community college remedial education is cost-effective.

The cost of remedial education is almost always grossly overestimated. When people hear that nearly one-third of college entrants require remedial education, they believe that one-third of college expenditures are spent on remedial education. This is not the case.

A number of national studies of the cost of remedial education have addressed total expenditures. For example, a Maryland study showed remedial expenditures of 1.2 percent of the higher education budget. A Texas study indicated that 2.2 percent of state higher education appropriations were spent on remedial programs. The most comprehensive study reported expenditures on remedial education at $1 billion of the United States higher education total

---

Why Should We Pay for It Twice?

Legislators often complain they have already paid high schools for work being repeated in community college remedial education. Yet, in most cases, remedial courses are not a repetition of high school course work.

- In nearly all states, a gap exists between competencies required for high school graduation and those required for college entry. A student can complete high school requirements and not be fully prepared to begin college.

- High school tracking systems still place more than half their students in outdated general or occupational curriculums that do not prepare them for college or information-age employment.

- Students from low-income families often begin school well behind, have inadequate home support, and are still behind when they enter community college.

- There are individuals not ready to put in the necessary effort until they have had a few years of life experience. Many students enter community college 10 years or more after high school. For them, remedial courses are a skill refresher.

expenditures of $115 billion, or approximately 1 percent (Breneman 1999). A U.S. General Accounting Office study showed that 4 percent of federal student financial aid was used for remedial education.

These expenditures are remarkably low when, in community colleges alone, more than a million students per year benefit. Each year, a half-million students complete remedial education successfully and continue on the road to productive lives through an expenditure of only 1 percent of the higher education budget. Expenditures per student are even more revealing. Half of community college remedial education students take six semester credits or fewer of remedial course work, and more than 80 percent take 12 semester credits or fewer. The average, 7.7 semester credits, is equivalent to one-quarter of a college year.

Using a high expenditure figure of $7,000 per community college full-time-equivalent student and a 75 percent public share, the average public expenditure per remedial student would be $1,312. Since 40 to 50 percent of students are successfully remediated, using the high expenditure estimate, the cost for each success would be between $2,624 and $3,280. The cost-effectiveness of remedial education is apparent when compared with expenditures on other programs. The nation's prison population has grown to the highest per capita in the world—1.1 million in jail and 5.5 million under corrections supervision (Harlow 1998). Each prisoner generates an expense of $25,000 to $35,000 per year. Ten students can have the foundation for their future built through remedial education for the same cost as incarcerating one person for a single year. Remedial programs are a far more productive use of public funds. Supporting community college remedial programs is cost-effective public policy.

Finding 10. Mathematics is the greatest hurdle for deficient students. Mathematics requirements need to be carefully reviewed.

The debate continues over mathematics expectations for standard college class work. From state to state and test to test, substantial differences exist.

Generally, mathematics faculty, rather than the faculty as a whole, determine the competencies to be tested. The question of what skills are needed for most college classes is seldom a consideration, nor is the question of what mathematics competencies are necessary as life skills.

Sixty-two percent of remedial education students are deficient in mathematics, compared with 37.7 percent in reading and 44.6 percent in writing. The figure for mathematics is too high. Either adjustments in expectations or major improvements in high school preparation are needed—perhaps both. A considerable amount of work has been done to identify 21st-century employment skills. A high percentage of successful remedial education students go into occupational programs or directly to work. It would therefore be beneficial to invite business and industry leaders to help identify the mathematics components of community college remedial education programs.

Finding 11. Present outcome measures do not produce useful data.

Remedial education programs are constructed with the goal of preparing students for bachelor's degrees. Program effectiveness most often is measured by the number of degrees earned. Student

The Public Supports Maximum Opportunity

Many legislators fail to understand the importance of remedial education in maintaining essential opportunities for youth. They misread the strong public belief in access to higher education and support for those in need of additional help. As demonstrated in a recent national poll conducted by the Public Agenda Foundation on a commission from the National Center for Higher Education and Public Policy, public belief indicates that:

- College education had become as important as a high school diploma (87 percent).
- College is more important than it was 10 years ago (84 percent).
- It is not possible for the United States to have too many college-educated individuals (76 percent).
- It is certain or very likely that their children will go to college (white 72.4 percent, African American 74 percent, Hispanic 70.9 percent).
- Learning high-tech skills is absolutely essential (67 percent), or important (29 percent).
- Students who fall behind should be provided with extra help, such as tutoring (white 94.5 percent, African American 98.4 percent, Hispanic 99.3 percent).
- Additional support should be provided to those who fall behind even if it is because of slacking off (white 67.5 percent, African American 83.5 percent, Hispanic 74.5 percent).

follow-up is difficult, and evaluators do not want to wait many years for results. Therefore, outcomes are typically evaluated after three or four years for associate degrees and five or six years for bachelor's degrees. Such evaluation produces results that do not coordinate with student behavior and often give the inaccurate impression that remedial programs are failing.

Most community college students are employed, often full time. They must arrange studies around job and personal obligations. They frequently skip terms or reduce loads. These students often take five or more years to complete an associate degree. Measuring community college students three years after admission finds few graduates, especially among students who need to take remedial courses before beginning a regular curriculum.

The majority of remedial education students gain skills and go directly to work or proceed to occupational certificates and degrees. This is a constructive result for society and is completely missed in current outcome evaluations.

We should continue to explore practical ways to follow up with students to learn how many achieve degrees. However, positive life results and varied paths for successful students make completion of remedial education the most important and useful measure of the success of remedial programs.

Finding 12. Mandatory testing and placement is an essential component of remedial education programs.

If community colleges do not know which students are academically underprepared, they have no way to provide appropriate programs. It is unfair to students to permit them to enroll in courses for which they are not prepared. Open enrollment in courses produces a spread of competencies that seriously handicaps the ability of faculty to provide effective education. In practice, either large numbers of students drop out or fail, or expectations are lowered to accommodate those who are unprepared for course work.

In the 1960s, college access was expanded, and students were allowed to make their own course choices without restriction. Consistent with attitudes of the time, colleges operated on the basis that students knew their strengths and limitations best and should have "the right to fail." In other words, colleges let them try anything, whether the students were adequately prepared or not.

By the early 1970s, it became apparent that this unrestricted approach was a failure, and colleges began to adjust their policies. Miami-Dade Community College, for example, undertook comprehensive educational reform. When students did not succeed, the college intervened and imposed load restrictions and implemented other supporting policies. Mandatory assessment and placement were at the center of reform. The reform resulted in the reestablishment of college standards and higher completion and retention rates, especially for minorities. The experience sparked a national movement toward mandatory assessment and mandatory placement.

Many researchers have addressed this issue and found that sound educational practice demands mandatory assessment and mandatory placement. John and Suanne Roueche have studied community college remedial programs for more than 20 years. They found that "information from colleges that make assessment and placement mandatory, together with data reporting the performance of all students taking remedial work, suggest that remediation correlates with improved performance over the rest of the college experience." In addition, "Colleges in states that require assessment and placement report that student retention and success levels improved when mandatory policies were enforced" (Roueche and Roueche 1999, 47). When deficient students are not required to enroll in remedial education courses, community colleges universally report that a significant number do not. A study by K. Patricia Cross found that fewer than 10 percent of those needing but not enrolling in remedial education survived in college (Cross 1976).

Those who oppose mandatory placement believe that motivation is essential to success, and in order to be motivated, students must self-select their courses. Although motivation is important, self-selection is not the only way for it to be achieved. In this study, a number of students indicated that they did not understand why they were required to enroll in remedial courses and

---

Customize Remedial Programs

Programs for underprepared students should be customized to the greatest degree possible. Wide variations exist in the competencies of underprepared students, from a student who is seriously deficient in all areas of remedial education to one who may be deficient in a single competency. Sound policy requires students who are deficient across the board to complete remedial work before beginning regular college courses, because they need to concentrate their efforts. Those with limited deficiencies, however, are best off combining needed remedial services with college courses for which they are prepared.

---

felt "trapped." These responses were clustered in certain colleges. It is the responsibility of community colleges to encourage students and help them to understand the value of remedial course requirements.

Mandatory assessment and mandatory placement are at the core of effective remedial programs.

Finding 13. Most community colleges fail to use the substantial research concerning successful remedial education.

In most community colleges, remedial education is not given the priority or support commensurate with its importance to the United States. Helping underprepared students may be the most important service that community colleges can render to our country. Effective remedial education is an essential bridge in this effort. Yet remedial programs are not recognized for their importance and are systematically undersupported.

In institutions staffed by highly educated individuals with a strong interest in intellectual pursuits, it is natural to want to concentrate on "the best and the brightest." College faculty often shun remedial education. Legislators disparage the programs and view them as a detriment to standards. For those not directly involved, it is hard to understand that an institution can have open-door admission and still retain high expectations for program graduates. It is easy to understand why community college presidents often fail to publicly advocate remedial programs.

Some cynics have called remedial education the community college's dirty little secret. The lack of priority translates into continuing practices that are old, inexpensive, and easy to administer. Thirty years of research have provided a substantial body of knowledge to guide those who work with under-prepared students on community college campuses. The following techniques, models, or structures contribute to successful remediation:

- Implementation of mandatory assessment and placement
- Establishment of clearly specified goals and objectives for developmental programs and courses
- Use of mastery learning techniques in remedial courses
- Provision of a high degree of structure in remedial courses
- Use of a variety of approaches and methods in remedial instruction
- Application of sound cognitive theory in the design and delivery of remedial courses
- Provision of a centralized or highly coordinated remedial program
- Use of a formative evaluation to guide program development and improvements
- Establishment of a strong philosophy of learning to develop program goals and objectives and to deliver program services
- Provision of a counseling component integrated into the structure of remedial education
- Provision of tutoring performed by well-trained tutors
- Integration of classroom and laboratory activities
- Establishment of an institutionwide commitment to remediation
- Assurance of consistency between exit standards for remedial courses and entry standards for regular curriculum
- Use of learning communities in remedial instruction
- Use of supplemental instruction, particularly video based
- Provision of supplemental instruction to support remedial courses
- Provision of courses or workshops on strategic thinking
- Provision of staff training and professional development for those who work with underprepared students
- Provision of ongoing student orientation courses
- Integration of critical thinking into the remedial curriculum

A New Image for Remedial Education

Without doubt, student attitudes toward their programs are a key to learning success. This is especially the case for academically deficient students. They have usually had a failing experience in high school, are filled with self-doubt, and frequently have low self-esteem. They need to work with staff who believe in them and help them understand that they are engaged in important work. The term *remedial* definitely has a negative connotation that fuels self-doubt. Some community colleges use the term *developmental*, Florida uses *college preparatory*, and there are numerous other constructive terms that better describe programs for underprepared individuals.

In recent years, some exciting and effective remedial programs have been developed. Nevertheless, the information concerning effective practices has been largely ignored. Only 6 of the 25 study colleges reported significant remedial program revision in the past 10 years.

Providing effective remedial education is not a mysterious proposition. We know how to do it. We simply do not use what we know.

4

RECOMMENDATIONS TO PUBLIC DECISION-MAKERS AND COMMUNITY COLLEGE LEADERS

The future of American business is in information-based industries. Knowledge multiplies competencies and results in greater productivity. In a world economy, U.S. workers need to be more productive to offset lower wages in less-developed countries and to support an aging population. To meet these challenges, the United States needs a broadly based, highly skilled workforce.

Eighty percent of new jobs will require some college. Yet less than half of our youth are prepared to begin college. Aggressive public school reforms are underway throughout the country, but gains will not come quickly or easily. Educators face a daunting task. Minorities will soon be a majority of our youth, and they are disproportionately behind in education. The evolving educational pattern is a continuum that includes college entry. Many will not be prepared. They will depend on community college remedial education as a lifeline to their future.

The recommendations that follow are directed primarily at public decision-makers and community college leaders and are intended to strengthen remedial programs in the new U.S. educational chain.

GENERAL RECOMMENDATIONS

Recommendation 1. Community college remedial education must be included in all long-term educational plans.

- To be competitive in the evolving global economy, the United States must have a highly skilled workforce. We must fully develop all of our human resources.

- The percentage of individuals in their prime work years will decline sharply and skills required for employment will continue to rise.

- All segments of the population that are growing most quickly are disproportionately underprepared. Because of persistent poverty and changes in demographics, immigration, and the American family, increased percentages of children will not be prepared to begin their education.

- The task for public schools is increasingly difficult. Despite progress in school reform, substantial percentages of Americans will reach adulthood without the skills and competencies required for 21st-century employment.

- Currently, 84 percent of young Americans graduate from high school, but only 67 percent graduate with a standard diploma. Seventy percent of the graduates eventually enter higher education, but almost a third are underprepared. The result is a significant gap between the skills of young Americans and those needed for the 80 percent of new jobs that require some postsecondary education.

- For underprepared adults, community college remedial education is the primary bridge to continued education, constructive employment, and full participation in society.

- Community college remedial education is essential to America's well-being.

Recommendation 2. Legislatures must provide financial support for community college remedial education at a level commensurate with its importance to the United States.

Recommendation 3. Community colleges must give remedial education higher priority and greater support.

- Neither legislatures nor community colleges support remedial programs sufficiently to ensure success.

- Research shows that underprepared students require more personal attention. They often have personal, job, and family issues that must be addressed if there is to be academic progress. Successful remedial education is more than courses; it is a program integrated into all college services. For these reasons, remedial education requires more resources than standard academic courses.

- Most states fund remedial education at the same or lower rates than standard academic programs. As a result, resources available are insufficient to support desired results.

- Community colleges have some latitude in appropriating funds to programs. Although a number of community colleges address the special needs of remedial programs, most do not.

- Institutional commitment to underprepared students is of greatest importance. Successful remediation occurs in direct proportion to priority given to the program by the college. Most important is a caring staff who believe in the students and in the importance of their work. Presidential leadership, in word and deed, is critical to success.

Recommendation 4. Because of the exceptional cost/benefits ratio community college remedial education provides, it should have a primary role in state and college educational plans.

- Each year, nearly a third of students who enter higher education are academically underprepared, and more than a million students enroll in community college remedial education. Half a million students are successfully remediated.

- Typically, the average full-time-equivalent expenditure on remedial courses is less than that for other community college courses.

- Less than 1 percent of U.S. higher education budgets and less than 4 percent of federal financial aid is spent on remedial education.

- The cost per remedial student is approximately 25 percent of the annual cost for a community college education, or a fraction of the annual cost of a four-year college education.

Recommendation 5. The continued and substantial lag in educational progress for minorities demands massive reform.

- To fulfill the promise of a just and compassionate nation, all American citizens must have the opportunity to fully develop their talents.

- As the United States is transformed by the information age, the academic skills that people need have escalated, leaving substantial numbers of minorities underprepared.

- By 2020, a majority of American children will be nonwhite. The nation's future depends on these children developing into a well-educated, highly skilled workforce.

- The gap in the educational progress of minorities is dramatic. Compared with white non-Hispanics, African Americans have half the chance of receiving a bachelor's degree, and Hispanics have only one-third the chance. Minorities lose ground at each successive level of education.

RECOMMENDATIONS FOR ASSESSMENT AND EVALUATION

Recommendation 6. Mandatory assessment and mandatory placement should be required of all entering students. If a state fails to require assessment and placement, the community colleges should.

- If the college does not know a student is deficient, it cannot provide an appropriate program.

- It is unfair to students and undermines program quality if students are allowed to enroll in courses for which they are underprepared and have little prospect of success.

- Few students who are academically deficient and fail to enroll in remedial education are academically successful.

Recommendation 7. An assessment program linked to educational prescriptions should be instituted. Assessments, however, must go beyond just identifying those who are deficient. They must also provide the basis for learning solutions.

- Today, the capability exists to develop diagnostic assessment of specific academic competencies and deficiencies. The College Board and ACT are developing diagnostic assessment instruments.

- Developments in information technology are making it possible and practical to individualize student learning programs.

- The ability to link diagnostic assessment to educational prescriptions and to individualize learning programs holds promise for important gains in learning and justifies a significant investment.

Recommendation 8. Community colleges should create a coordinated, seamless transition from high school to college.

Recommendation 9. High school assessment and college-placement programs should be integrated into a seamless assessment system. High schools, and high school students themselves, need to know how the students are progressing in developing college-entry skills.

- Educational underpreparation develops early in life. The sooner intervention is initiated, the better the prospects for overcoming educational deficiencies.

- Education beyond high school is becoming almost universal. In order to provide appropriate educational programs, the progress of students in mastering college-entry skills should be assessed while they are still in high school.

- In most states, the minimum skills required for high school graduation are not equivalent to those required for college entry.

- Too many high school students complete graduation requirements early in their senior year and believe they are prepared for college entry, even if they are not. Their senior year, therefore, is often wasted.

- Community colleges with successful entry programs work with high schools to prepare students for the transition to college. Such programs reduce the number of underprepared students and increase the number who successfully continue their education.

- The educational system, including assessment programs, should be a seamless continuum.

Recommendation 10. Successful completion of remedial education is the most important program outcome. It should be the primary measure of program evaluation and funding.

- Evaluation based on degrees earned should continue. The most useful gauge of remedial program effectiveness, however, is successful completion, which is the most critical achievement in personal development.

- Fewer than 1 in 6 successful remedial education students earn an academic associate degree or bachelor's degree. More than one-third, however, earn an occupational associate degree or certificate.

- Nine years after students complete remedial education, 98.5 percent are employed and 90 percent work in jobs above entry or unskilled levels. Most of these individuals are in information-based positions for which there is high demand. Only 2 percent of these individuals have been convicted of a felony. These results are dramatically better than those for a general population of comparable demographics.

- Successful remedial education students experience positive life developments after completing a remedial program.

- Following successful remediation, underprepared students do as well in college-level courses as do students who entered college academically prepared.

PROGRAM RECOMMENDATIONS

Recommendation 11. Services for underprepared students must fully use the knowledge gained from successful remedial education programs.

- Research has provided substantial insight into how underprepared students learn.

- Exemplary remedial education programs should serve as models.

- Many community colleges ignore available knowledge and continue to deliver services in undersupported, traditional arrangements.

- Doing less than our best is unacceptable.

Recommendation 12. New programs for seriously deficient students must be developed that are unique in their organization and delivery. While not closing opportunity for students to move upward, they should have unique goals.

- The composition of seriously deficient students (those deficient in all basic skills and having lower-level skills in at least one category) differs sharply from other academically deficient students. Whereas seriously deficient students are 75 percent minority, other deficient students are 60 percent white non-Hispanic. And while 1 in 5 minority remedial students are seriously deficient, only white non-Hispanic remedial students are seriously deficient.

- Only 20 percent of seriously deficient students were successfully remediated, in contrast to 43 percent of other deficient students.

- Fewer than 5 percent of seriously deficient students earned more than 20 credits at their community college. Fewer than 2 percent earned a bachelor's degree.

- Programs for the seriously deficient are unsuccessful.

Recommendation 13. With adequate funding, community colleges should be able to increase the percentage of students who are successfully remediated as well as the percentage who proceed to four-year degrees.

- Increased remedial completion rates are an important program goal.

- Despite positive outcomes for those who successfully complete remedial education, a significantly greater number should earn four-year degrees. In the information-age economy, opportunities abound for professionally educated individuals.

- Remedial education students are more often from minority background, and in the United States, minorities are substantially underrepresented in professional fields. The knowledge of how to improve results, with appropriate resources, is available.

Recommendation 14. A national guide should be instituted to assist community colleges in developing appropriate and effective remedial education programs.

- It is essential for our nation's future that a higher percentage of young adults gain the skills necessary for employment. Too many people are being lost.

- Most programs for seriously deficient students are unsuccessful and need a full revision.

- Business and industry representatives should be involved in developing the guide. A high percentage of successful remedial education students go into occupational programs or into the workplace. Skills needed to begin standard college work and those needed for information-age job entry are similar.

- Mathematics is a major hurdle for remedial education students. Goals in this discipline require careful review.

BIBLIOGRAPHY

Blau, Francine D., and Marianne A. Ferber. 1986. *The Economics of Women, Men, and Work*. Englewood Cliffs, N.J.: Prentice Hall.

Breneman, David W. 1999. "Remediation in Higher Education: Its Extent and Cost." In *Brookings Paper on Education Policy*, ed. D. Ravitch. Washington D.C.: Brookings Institution.

Carnevale, Anthony P. 1996. "Liberal Education and the New Economy." *Liberal Education* 82, 2: 4–11.

Carnevale, Anthony P., and Donna M. Desrochers. 1999. "Getting Down to Business: Matching Welfare Recipients' Skills to Jobs that Train." Princeton: Educational Testing Service.

Cross, K. 1976. *Accent on Learning*. San Francisco: Jossey-Bass.

Durand, John D. 1968. *The Labor Force in the United States, 1890–1960*. New York: Gordon and Breach.

Education Trust. 1998. *Education Watch: The Education Trust 1998 State and National Data Book*. Washington, D.C.: Education Trust.

Fallon, Joseph E. 1996. "The Impact of Immigration on U.S. Demographics." *Journal of Social, Political and Economic Studies* 21, 2 (summer): 144–167.

Federman, Maya, et al. 1996. "What Does It Mean to Be Poor in America?" *Monthly Labor Review* (May): 3–15.

Friedman, Dorian, and Kenan Pollack. 1996. "Ahead: A Very Different Nation." *U.S. News and World Report* (25 March): 16.

Gordon, David M., Richard Edwards, and Michael Reich. 1982. *Segmented Work, Divided Workers: The Historical Transformation of Labor in the United States*. Cambridge, England: Cambridge University Press.

Greenberg, Eric. 1997. *Skill Standards: Benchmarks of Excellence*. Washington, D.C.: National Alliance of Business.

Harlow, Caroline Wolf. 1998. "Profile of Jail Inmates, 1996." Washington, D.C.: U.S. Government Printing Office.

Hickman, Randall C., and John W. Quinley. 1997. "A Synthesis of Local, State, and National Studies in Workforce Education and Training." In *Core Issues in Community Colleges.* Washington, D.C.: American Association of Community Colleges.

Hill, Lewis E. 1998. "The Institutional Economics of Poverty: An Inquiry into the Cause and Effect of Poverty." *Journal of Economic Issues* (June).

Hodgkinson, Harold L. 1997. "Diversity Comes in All Sizes and Shapes." *School Business Affairs* (April): 3–9.

———. 1998. "Demographics of Diversity for the 21st Century." *Education Digest* (October): 4–7.

———. 1999. *All One System: A Second Look. Perspectives in Public Policy: Connecting Higher Education and the Public Schools.* Washington, D.C.: Institute for Educational Leadership and National Center for Public Policy and Higher Education.

Jet. 1996. (30 December): 32.

Leland, John, and Gregory Beals. 1997. "In Living Colors." *Newsweek*, 5 May: 58–60.

Lichter, Daniel. 1997. "Poverty and Inequality among Children." *Annual Review of Sociology:* 121–146.

Marshall, Ray, and Marc Tucker. 1992. *Thinking for a Living: Work, Skills, and the Future of the American Economy.* New York: Basic Books.

Morganthau, Tom. 1997. "The Face of the Future." *Newsweek* (27 January): 58–60.

National Center for Education Statistics. 1998. *Digest of Education Statistics.* Washington, D.C.: U.S. Department of Education.

———. 2000. Education Enrollment Trends. Unpublished report.

Peterson, Peter G. 1996. "Will America Grow Up Before It Grows Old?" *Atlantic Monthly* (May).

Peyser, Marc. 1999. "Home of the Gray." *Newsweek* (1 March): 50–53.

Preston, Samuel. 1999. "Children Will Pay. Demography's Crystal Ball Shows That 21st-Century America Will Be Older, Wiser, and More Ethnically Diverse. But Kids Face Trouble." *New York Times Magazine* (29 September): 96–97.

Roueche, John D., and Suanne E. Roueche. 1999. *High Stakes, High Performance: Making Remedial Education Work.* Washington, D.C.: Community College Press, American Association of Community Colleges.

Saxon, D. Patrick, and Hunter R Boylan. 2000. "Issues in Community College Remedial Education." Working manuscript. Miami, Fla.: League for Innovation in the Community College.

Sivy, Michael. 1997. "What America Will Look Like in 25 Years." *Money* (October): 98–102.

"Social Science and the Citizen." 1996. *Society* (July/August): 3–5.

Soul, Ralph S. 1998. "On Connecting School and Work." *The Annals of the American Academy of Political and Social Science* (September): 168–175.

Statistical Abstracts of the United States. 1973. U.S. Department of Commerce. Washington, D.C.: U.S. Government Printing Office.

U.S. Bureau of the Census. 1975. *Historical Statistics of the United States: Colonial Time to 1970.* Part 1, 137, 139. Washington, D.C.: U.S. Government Printing Office.

———. 1997. "Table 649: Employment by Industry: 1970 to 1996." In *Statistical Abstract of the United States*, 415. Washington, D.C.: U.S. Government Printing Office.

———. 1999. "Table 2.1: Population Trends." In *Statistical Abstracts*, 20. Washington, D.C.: U.S. Government Printing Office.

U.S. Bureau of Labor Statistics. Series D 127-141. *Employees on Nonagricultural Payrolls, by Major Industry Divisions: 1900 to 1970.* Washington, D.C.: Bureau of Labor Statistics.

———. Series D 152-166. *Industrial Distribution of Gainful Workers: 1920 to 1940.* Washington, D.C.: Bureau of Labor Statistics.

———. Series D 167-181. *Labor Force and Employment, by Industry: 1800 to 1960.* Washington, D.C.: Bureau of Labor Statistics.

U.S. Department of Commerce, et al. 1999. *21st-Century Skills for 21st-Century Jobs.* Washington, D.C.: U.S. Government Printing Office.

U.S. Department of Justice, Office of Justice Programs. 1998. *Correctional Populations in the United States in 1996*. Washington, D.C.: U.S. Government Printing Office.

U.S. Department of Justice, Office of Policy and Planning. 1998. *Legal Immigration, Fiscal Year 1998*. Washington, D.C.: U.S. Government Printing Office.

Weinberg, Daniel. 1998. Press briefing on 1997 income and poverty estimates. Washington, D.C.: U.S. Bureau of the Census.

White, Jack. 1997. "I'm Just Who I Am." *Time* (5 May).

INDEX

ABOUT THE AUTHOR

Robert McCabe is senior fellow with the League for Innovation in the Community College and former president of Miami-Dade Community College. In 40 years as a leader in higher education, he has been a consistent and forceful advocate for underprepared students. McCabe has written more than 100 articles, monographs, and books. His most ambitious project is the recently completed National Study of Community College Remedial Education, the basis for this report. McCabe has served on more than 70 educational boards, including the National Center for Public Policy and Higher Education, and he is a recipient of the American Association of Community College's Leadership Award.